Welcome to Belgrade, the capital and largest city of Serbia, located at the confluence of two major European rivers, the Danube and the Sava. Belgrade has a rich history, dating back over two millennia, and has been influenced by various cultures and empires throughout its past. Today, it is a modern city with a vibrant nightlife, diverse cuisine, and a multitude of cultural and historical attractions to explore.

In this travel guide, we will provide you with all the information you need to make the most of your trip to Belgrade. From the city's top landmarks and museums, to its best restaurants and cafes, to its lively nightlife and entertainment scene, we have got you covered. We will also offer practical advice on transportation, currency, safety, and more, to ensure that your stay in Belgrade is as enjoyable and stress-free as possible.

So sit back, relax, and let us take you on a journey through this beautiful and fascinating city.

Contents

I. Introduction to Belgrade...5

    A. Brief History 5

    B. Culture and People..7

    C. Climate and Best Time to Visit 8

II. Getting to Belgrade 10

    A. By Air...10

    B. By Train 12

    C. By Bus...14

III. Transportation within Belgrade 17

    A. Public Transportation..17

    B. Taxis and Ride-Sharing 19

    C. Biking and Walking 20

IV. Accommodation in Belgrade 23

    A. Hotels...23

    B. Hostels and Guesthouses 24

    C. Vacation Rentals..25

    D. Our recommended hotel: Hotel Moskva 25

V. Sightseeing and Attractions 27

    A. Historical Landmarks...27

    B. Museums and Galleries...29

    C. Parks and Outdoor Spaces 31

    D. Unique Experiences 33

VI. Food and Dining..37

    A. Serbian Cuisine..37

B. Restaurants and Cafes...39

C. Vegetarian and Vegan Options 41

VII. Nightlife and Entertainment.................................43

A. Clubs and Bars...43

B. Live Music Venues..45

C. Cultural Events and Festivals.................................45

VIII. Shopping in Belgrade 47

A. Shopping Malls..47

B. Local Markets 47

C. Souvenir and Specialty Shops................................48

IX. Practical Information..49

X. Day Trips from Belgrade...51

Our 3-Day Travel Itinerary to Belgrade 59

Day 1 in Belgrade: Arrival, Walk and Monuments ...59

ZoomTip 1.3 Information on the Monuments 63

Who is Nikola Tesla 67

The Residence of Knjeginja Ljubica 69

Who is Ivo Andric 70

Day 2 in Belgrade: Shopping and Sightseeing 73

Day 2 in Belgrade: Map 74

ZoomTip 2.1 Try the Karadjordje's steak..................77

Day 3 in Belgrade: City's Museums and Memorable Figures 78

ZoomTip 3.1 Taxi Fares in Belgrade...........................81

Thank you..84

I. Introduction to Belgrade

A. Brief History

Belgrade, the capital of Serbia, boasts a rich and fascinating history that spans over 2,000 years. The city has been settled, conquered, and rebuilt multiple times throughout its existence, bearing witness to the rise and fall of various empires, kingdoms, and republics. With its strategic location at the confluence of the Sava and Danube rivers, Belgrade has been a critical center of power, trade, and culture in the Balkan region.

The earliest known settlements in the area date back to the Neolithic period, around 6,000 BCE. However, the first significant urban development occurred in the 3rd century BCE, when the Celtic tribe Scordisci established a fortified settlement known as Singidunum. Later, in the 1st century CE, the Romans conquered the area and further developed the city, incorporating it into the province of Moesia. During the Roman period, Singidunum became an essential military outpost, protecting the empire's border along the Danube.

Over the centuries that followed, the city was repeatedly besieged and conquered by various barbarian tribes, including the Huns, Sarmatians, and Avars. In the 6th century, the Byzantine Empire annexed Singidunum, renaming it Beligrad, which means "White City" in Slavic languages. This name eventually evolved into the modern Serbian name Beograd or Belgrade in English.

Throughout the Middle Ages, Belgrade remained a contested area, as various powers vied for control of the city. In 1166, it became the capital of the medieval Serbian state under Stefan Nemanja, the founder of the Nemanjić dynasty. However, the Byzantine Empire, the Kingdom of Hungary, and later the Ottoman Empire all laid claim to the city at various points in time.

The Ottoman Empire first captured Belgrade in 1521, marking the beginning of a nearly four-century-long period of Ottoman rule. During this time, Belgrade became a significant administrative and military center within the empire. The city experienced a significant transformation, as its population and infrastructure expanded, and its cultural landscape shifted to reflect its new rulers.

In 1804, the First Serbian Uprising erupted against the Ottoman Empire, resulting in the creation of the modern Serbian state. After several failed attempts, the Serbian forces, led by Prince Miloš Obrenović, successfully expelled the Ottomans from Belgrade in 1867, making the city the capital of the Principality of Serbia. In 1882, Serbia was declared a kingdom, with Belgrade remaining the capital.

Throughout the late 19th and early 20th centuries, Belgrade continued to grow in size and importance, establishing itself as a critical center of politics, culture, and education in the Balkans. In 1918, following the end of World War I, Belgrade became the capital of the newly formed Kingdom of Serbs, Croats, and Slovenes, which was later renamed the Kingdom of Yugoslavia in 1929.

During World War II, Belgrade was occupied by the Axis powers, suffering significant destruction from both German bombing campaigns and the ensuing Yugoslav Partisan resistance. After the war, the city was rebuilt, and Belgrade became the capital of the newly established Socialist Federal Republic of Yugoslavia, led by Josip Broz Tito.

Throughout the second half of the 20th century, Belgrade continued to expand and develop, becoming a prominent center of industry, science, and culture within Yugoslavia. However, the city also faced challenges, as political tensions and economic struggles plagued the country. In the 1990s, the disintegration of Yugoslavia led to a series of conflicts known as the Yugoslav Wars. Belgrade suffered significant damage during the 1999 NATO bombing campaign in response to the Kosovo War. This period marked a dark chapter in the city's history, as its infrastructure was heavily damaged, and many lives were lost.

Following the wars, Serbia and Montenegro formed a new union in 2003, with Belgrade as its capital. In 2006, Montenegro voted for independence, leading to the establishment of the Republic of Serbia, with Belgrade remaining the capital city.

Since then, Belgrade has embarked on a path of recovery and renewal. The city has experienced significant growth, attracting both foreign and domestic investment. Its population has become increasingly diverse, and the city has evolved into a vibrant, cosmopolitan hub that draws visitors from around the world.

B. Culture and People

Belgrade's rich history has shaped its unique cultural landscape, which reflects the city's diverse and multicultural past. The city's architecture is a testament to its complex history, with buildings that span various styles and periods, from Ottoman, Austro-Hungarian, and Socialist to modern designs.

The people of Belgrade are known for their warm hospitality and friendly demeanor. Serbs are generally very proud of their country, culture, and history. They are eager to share their customs, traditions, and stories with visitors, making travelers feel welcome and at home.

Belgrade has a vibrant arts and culture scene, with numerous theaters, galleries, and cultural institutions throughout the city. Some notable venues include the National Theatre, the Yugoslav Drama Theatre, and the Belgrade Philharmonic Orchestra. The city also hosts numerous festivals and cultural events, such as the Belgrade International Theatre Festival (BITEF), the Belgrade International Documentary Film Festival (Beldocs), and the Belgrade Dance Festival.

In recent years, Belgrade's contemporary art scene has flourished, with a growing number of galleries, studios, and creative spaces. The Savamala district, in particular, has emerged as a hub of contemporary art and culture, featuring numerous galleries, workshops, and creative spaces.

C. Climate and Best Time to Visit

Belgrade has a continental climate, with four distinct seasons. Summers in the city are generally hot and humid, with temperatures ranging from 20°C (68°F) to 30°C (86°F), and occasional heatwaves that can push temperatures above 35°C (95°F). Winters are cold and often snowy, with temperatures that can drop below freezing, especially during January and February.

The best time to visit Belgrade is during the spring (April-May) or fall (September-October) when the weather is milder and more pleasant. During these months, temperatures typically range from 15°C (59°F) to 25°C (77°F), making it an ideal time for sightseeing and outdoor activities.

However, if you prefer a more lively atmosphere, consider visiting during the summer months when the city's parks, outdoor cafes, and riverbanks come alive with people enjoying the warm weather. Keep in mind that this is also the peak tourist season, so popular attractions may be more crowded, and accommodation prices might be higher.

In summary, Belgrade is a captivating city with a complex history that has shaped its diverse and vibrant culture. Its unique blend of architectural styles, welcoming people, and dynamic arts scene make it an exciting destination for travelers to explore. Whether you're interested in history, art, or simply soaking up the atmosphere of this lively city, there's something for everyone to enjoy in Belgrade.

II. Getting to Belgrade

A. By Air

1. Belgrade Nikola Tesla Airport

Belgrade Nikola Tesla Airport (BEG) is the primary international gateway to the city and the largest and busiest airport in Serbia. Located about 18 km (11 miles) west of the city center, the airport serves as a hub for both domestic and international flights.

The airport offers various facilities and services for travelers, including ATMs, currency exchange offices, free Wi-Fi, a post office, luggage storage, and a lost and found office. There are also several dining options, such as restaurants, cafes, and fast-food outlets, as well as shops, duty-free stores, and a pharmacy.

Ground transportation options from the airport to the city center include:

- *Airport Shuttle (A1):* Operated by the public transport company GSP Beograd, the A1 shuttle runs between the airport and Slavija Square in the city center. Buses depart approximately every 20 minutes during the day and every hour during the night. A one-way ticket costs 300 RSD (about 2.5 EUR) and can be purchased from the driver or at the kiosk near the shuttle stop. The journey takes about 30-40 minutes, depending on traffic.

- *Public Bus Line 72:* Another option is the public bus line 72, which connects the airport with Zeleni Venac, a central bus hub in Belgrade. Buses run every 30 minutes during the day and every hour during the night. A one-way ticket costs 150 RSD (about 1.3 EUR) when purchased at a kiosk or 180 RSD (about 1.5 EUR) when purchased from the driver. The trip takes approximately 40-60 minutes, depending on traffic.

- *Taxis:* The airport has a taxi service counter in the baggage claim area, where you can get a voucher with a fixed price for your destination. Official airport taxis are marked with a blue "Airport Taxi" sign on the roof. A taxi ride to the city center costs around 1,800 RSD (about 15 EUR) and takes 20-30 minutes, depending on traffic. It's essential to use only official taxis to avoid potential scams.

- *Car Rental:* Several car rental companies operate at the airport, including Avis, Budget, Hertz, Enterprise, and Sixt. If you prefer the flexibility of driving yourself, you can book a car online or at the airport upon arrival.

2. Airlines and Flight Connections

Belgrade Nikola Tesla Airport is well-connected to many destinations in Europe, as well as a few cities in the Middle East, Africa, and North America. The national carrier, Air Serbia, operates flights to numerous European cities, such as London, Paris, Amsterdam, and Moscow, as well as long-haul destinations like New York and Toronto. Other major airlines serving Belgrade include Lufthansa, Turkish Airlines, Qatar Airways, KLM, and Austrian Airlines.

There are also several low-cost carriers that operate flights to and from Belgrade, including Wizz Air, Ryanair, easyJet, and Vueling. These airlines offer affordable connections to popular European cities like Barcelona, Milan, Berlin, and London.

It's essential to book your flights early, especially during the peak tourist season (June to September), to secure the best prices and availability. You can use flight comparison websites like Skyscanner, Kayak, or Google Flights to find the best deals on flights to

Belgrade. Keep in mind that flying with a low-cost carrier might mean additional fees for checked luggage, seat selection, or in-flight meals.

B. By Train
1. Belgrade Central Railway Station

In 2018, Belgrade's main railway station, known as Belgrade Center (Prokop), replaced the old central railway station. It is located approximately 4 km (2.5 miles) south of the city center. Although the new station is modern and well-equipped, it is not yet fully developed, and some amenities, like restaurants and shops, might be limited. However, you can find a ticket office, waiting area, restrooms, ATMs, and a small convenience store.

Ground transportation options from the railway station to the city center include:

- *Public Transportation:* Tram line 3 and bus line 36 connect Belgrade Center railway station with the city center. Tickets can be purchased at kiosks near the tram and bus stops and cost 150 RSD (about 1.3 EUR) for a single ride. The journey takes about 15-20 minutes, depending on traffic.

- *Taxis:* There is a taxi stand outside the railway station, and a ride to the city center should cost around 500 RSD (about 4.3 EUR) to 800 RSD (about 6.8 EUR), depending on the destination and traffic. Remember to use only official taxis to avoid potential scams.

2. International and Domestic Train Connections

Belgrade is well-connected to other cities in Serbia and neighboring countries by train. International train services operate between Belgrade and major European cities like Vienna, Budapest, Sofia, and Thessaloniki. These trains are generally slower and less frequent than flights, but they can be a more affordable and scenic option for travelers.

Some popular international train routes and approximate travel times include:

- Belgrade to Budapest: 8-9 hours

- Belgrade to Vienna: 11-12 hours

- Belgrade to Sofia: 9-10 hours

- Belgrade to Thessaloniki: 10-11 hours

You can book international train tickets online through the Serbian Railways website (https://www.srbvoz.rs/eng) or at the ticket office in Belgrade Center railway station. It's advisable to book your tickets in advance, especially during peak travel periods, to ensure availability.

Belgrade also serves as a hub for domestic train connections within Serbia. You can easily reach cities like Novi Sad, Niš, and Subotica by train. Some popular domestic train routes and approximate travel times include:

- Belgrade to Novi Sad: 2-2.5 hours

- Belgrade to Niš: 4-5 hours

- Belgrade to Subotica: 3-4 hours

Domestic train tickets can be purchased online through the Serbian Railways website, at the ticket office in the railway station, or on the train. However, buying tickets at the station or online is usually cheaper than purchasing them on the train.

Keep in mind that train services in Serbia can sometimes be slower and less reliable than in Western Europe, so it's essential to plan accordingly and be prepared for potential delays or schedule changes.

C. By Bus

1. Belgrade Bus Station

The main bus station in Belgrade is called the Belgrade Bus Station (BAS - Beogradska Autobuska Stanica). It is located near the city center, approximately 1.5 km (0.9 miles) from Republic Square. The bus station offers various facilities and services, including ticket offices, a waiting area, luggage storage, restrooms, ATMs, a currency exchange office, a small convenience store, and a café.

Ground transportation options from the bus station to the city center include:

- *Public Transportation:* Tram lines 2, 7, and 9, and bus lines 83, 27, and 37 connect the bus station with the city center. Tickets can be purchased at kiosks near the tram and bus stops and cost 150 RSD (about 1.3 EUR) for a single ride. The journey takes about 10-15 minutes, depending on traffic.

- *Taxis:* There is a taxi stand outside the bus station, and a ride to the city center should cost around 400 RSD (about 3.4 EUR) to 700 RSD (about 6 EUR), depending on the destination and traffic. Remember to use only official taxis to avoid potential scams.

2. Bus Companies and Routes

Belgrade is well-connected to other cities in Serbia and neighboring countries by bus. Traveling by bus can be an affordable and convenient alternative to trains or flights, especially for shorter distances or destinations not served by trains.

Some of the major bus companies operating in Belgrade include:

- Lasta (https://www.lasta.rs/en/)

- Niš-Ekspres (http://www.nis-ekspres.rs/en)

- Fudeks (https://www.fudeks.rs/en/)

These companies offer domestic and international bus routes, connecting Belgrade to cities like Novi Sad, Niš, and Subotica in Serbia, as well as Budapest, Vienna, Zagreb, Skopje, and Sarajevo in neighboring countries.

You can book bus tickets online through the bus companies' websites or at the ticket offices in the bus station. Some third-party websites, like Balkan Viator (https://www.balkanviator.com/en/bus-timetables) and BusTicket4.me (https://www.busticket4.me/EN/), also allow you to search for and book bus tickets across multiple companies.

It's advisable to book your tickets in advance, especially during peak travel periods, to ensure availability and secure the best prices. Keep in mind that bus services in the region can sometimes be slower and less reliable than in Western Europe, so it's essential to plan accordingly and be prepared for potential delays or schedule changes.

III. Transportation within Belgrade

A. Public Transportation

Public transportation in Belgrade is operated by GSP Beograd (http://www.gsp.rs/en) and consists of a network of buses, trams, and trolleybuses. The system is extensive and covers most parts of the city, making it a convenient and affordable way to get around.

1. *Buses*

Buses are the backbone of Belgrade's public transportation system, with numerous lines connecting different parts of the city. Buses generally run from 4:00 AM to midnight, with some lines operating 24 hours a day, known as night buses (marked with an "N" before the line number).

2. *Trams*

Belgrade's tram network consists of 12 lines that mainly serve the central and older parts of the city. Trams are generally slower than buses but can be a more scenic and enjoyable way to travel, particularly along the riverfront and through historic neighborhoods.

3. *Trolleybuses*

Trolleybuses are electric-powered buses that run on overhead wires. There are seven trolleybus lines in Belgrade, mainly serving the central and hilly areas of the city. Trolleybuses offer a quieter and more environmentally friendly alternative to regular buses.

Tickets and Fares

To use public transportation in Belgrade, you will need a contactless smart card called "BusPlus" (https://www.busplus.rs/eng). The card can be purchased at

BusPlus kiosks, newsstands, and post offices for 250 RSD (about 2.1 EUR). You can then load the card with credit or various types of passes, depending on your needs.

Fare options include:

- *Single ride ticket:* Costs 150 RSD (about 1.3 EUR) when purchased at a kiosk or 180 RSD (about 1.5 EUR) when purchased from the driver. It is valid for 90 minutes and allows for unlimited transfers between buses, trams, and trolleybuses during that time.

- *Daily pass:* Costs 350 RSD (about 3 EUR) and allows for unlimited travel on all modes of public transportation for 24 hours from the time of activation.

- *3-day pass:* Costs 750 RSD (about 6.4 EUR) and allows for unlimited travel on all modes of public transportation for 72 hours from the time of activation.

- *5-day pass:* Costs 1,000 RSD (about 8.5 EUR) and allows for unlimited travel on all modes of public transportation for 120 hours from the time of activation.

To use your BusPlus card, simply touch it to the electronic card reader when boarding a bus, tram, or trolleybus. If you need to transfer to another vehicle, touch your card to the reader again when boarding the new vehicle. Remember to always have your card ready, as ticket inspectors frequently check passengers for valid tickets.

Public transportation in Belgrade can sometimes be crowded, especially during rush hours, so be prepared for a less comfortable ride during these times. Nevertheless, the system offers an affordable and convenient way to explore the city and reach various attractions.

B. Taxis and Ride-Sharing
1. *Official Taxis*

Taxis are a convenient and relatively affordable way to get around Belgrade. However, it's essential to use only official taxis to avoid potential scams or overcharging. Official taxis have a "TX" mark on their license plates and a taxi sign on the roof. Some reliable taxi companies in Belgrade include:

- Lux Taxi (http://www.luxtaxi.co.rs/en/)

- Naxis Taxi (https://www.naxistaxi.com/en/)

- Pink Taxi (https://www.pinktaxi.rs/en/)

You can order a taxi by phone, using the taxi company's app, or hailing one on the street. It's generally better to order a taxi by phone or app, as the fare may be lower than when hailing one on the street. Taxi fares typically consist of a base fare (around 170 RSD or 1.5 EUR) and a per-kilometer charge (around 65 RSD or 0.6 EUR per kilometer). Tipping is not obligatory but appreciated for good service.

2. *Ride-Sharing Apps*

Ride-sharing services like Uber and Bolt are not currently operating in Belgrade. However, there are local alternatives available, such as Car:Go (https://www.appcargo.com/). Car:Go works similarly to Uber, allowing users to book rides using a smartphone app, with the fare being charged directly to their credit or debit card.

To use Car:Go, you will need to download the app and register for an account. Once your account is set up, you can request a ride by entering your pick-up location and destination. The app will then provide an estimated fare and wait time for your ride. Note that Car:Go prices can be slightly higher than regular taxis, but the service is generally more reliable and convenient.

When using taxis or ride-sharing services in Belgrade, it's essential to be aware of your surroundings and ensure that you are using a reputable company to avoid potential issues. Always check that the vehicle and driver match the information provided by the app or taxi company before getting into the car.

C. Biking and Walking
1. *Biking*

Belgrade is becoming increasingly bike-friendly, with an expanding network of bike lanes and paths, especially along the Sava and Danube rivers. Biking can be an enjoyable and healthy way to explore the city and its surroundings while taking in the sights.

There are several bike rental shops in Belgrade, offering a range of bicycles for rent, including city bikes, mountain bikes, and electric bikes. Some popular bike rental shops include:

- iBikeBelgrade (https://www.ibikebelgrade.com/)

- BG Bikes (https://www.bgbikes.rs/en/)

Rental rates typically start at around 1,000 RSD (about 8.5 EUR) per day for a city bike, with discounts available for multi-day rentals. Most rental shops will also provide helmets, locks, and maps upon request.

For a more organized biking experience, consider joining one of the guided bike tours offered by companies like iBikeBelgrade. These tours typically last for a few hours and cover various points of interest in the city, with knowledgeable guides providing insights into Belgrade's history and culture.

2. *Walking*

Walking is one of the best ways to explore Belgrade, particularly in the city center and historic neighborhoods like Stari Grad and Zemun. Many of the city's main attractions, such as Kalemegdan Fortress, the pedestrian street Knez Mihailova, and the bohemian district of Skadarlija, are best enjoyed on foot.

Belgrade's city center is relatively compact and walkable, with well-maintained sidewalks and pedestrian areas. However, be aware that some parts of the city can be hilly and may require a moderate level of fitness to navigate on foot.

For a more structured and informative walking experience, consider joining a guided walking tour. Several companies offer walking tours in Belgrade, covering various themes and areas of interest, such as:

- Belgrade Free Walking Tour (https://www.belgradefreetour.com/)

- Belgrade Walking Tours (https://belgradewalkingtours.com/)

These tours typically last for 2-3 hours and are led by knowledgeable local guides who can provide insights into Belgrade's history, culture, and everyday life. Some tours are free, operating on a "pay-what-you-want" basis, while others may have a fixed price.

Whether you choose to explore Belgrade by bike or on foot, both options offer a more immersive and environmentally friendly way to experience the city and its many attractions.

IV. Accommodation in Belgrade

A. Hotels

Belgrade offers a wide range of hotels to suit different budgets and preferences. From luxury hotels to budget options, you can find a comfortable place to stay during your visit to the city.

1. *Luxury Hotels*

For those seeking a more luxurious experience, Belgrade has several upscale hotels with top-notch amenities and services. Some popular luxury hotels in Belgrade include:

- Square Nine Hotel (https://www.squarenine.rs/): Located in the city center, this 5-star boutique hotel features elegantly designed rooms, a rooftop terrace, an indoor pool, and a spa.

- Hotel Metropol Palace (https://www.metropolpalace.com/): A historic hotel with modern amenities, it offers stylish rooms, a spa, an indoor pool, and a fine dining restaurant.

- Saint Ten Hotel (https://www.saintten.com/): A smaller, 5-star boutique hotel with a unique blend of historic charm and contemporary design, it offers personalized service and luxurious amenities.

2. *Mid-range Hotels*

If you're looking for a balance between comfort and affordability, there are numerous mid-range hotels in Belgrade. Some popular options include:

- Hotel Moskva (http://www.hotelmoskva.eu/): A historic hotel located on the famous Terazije Square, it offers comfortable rooms, a renowned café, and a spa.

- Mercure Belgrade Excelsior (https://all.accor.com/hotel/9674/index.en.shtml): A centrally located hotel with modern rooms and amenities, including a restaurant and bar.

- Hotel Park (https://www.hotelparkbeograd.rs/): Situated in a quiet area near the city center, this hotel offers comfortable rooms, a fitness center, and a restaurant.

3. *Budget Hotels*

For budget-conscious travelers, there are several affordable hotel options in Belgrade. Some popular budget hotels include:

- Hotel Slavija (https://www.slavijahotelbeograd.com/en/): A budget hotel with basic, functional rooms and a convenient location near the city center.

- Hotel Srbija (https://www.hotelsrbijagarni.com/en/): Located in a residential area, this hotel offers affordable rooms and easy access to public transportation.

- Hotel Opera (http://www.operahotel.rs/en/): A small, budget-friendly hotel with clean and comfortable rooms, located near the city center.

B. Hostels and Guesthouses

Hostels and guesthouses are an excellent option for budget travelers and those looking for a more social atmosphere. Belgrade has a vibrant hostel scene, with many options offering a mix of dorms and private rooms. Some popular hostels and guesthouses in Belgrade include:

- Hedonist Hostel (https://www.hedonisthostelbelgrade.com/): Located in a historic building in the city center, it offers a cozy atmosphere, a garden, and a variety of room types.

- Hostel Bongo (https://hostel-bongo-belgrade.booked.net/): A modern hostel with a colorful design, it features dorms and private rooms, a rooftop terrace, and a central location.

- Green House Hostel (http://www.greenhousebelgrade.com/): A small, eco-friendly hostel with a focus on sustainability, it offers comfortable accommodations and a welcoming atmosphere.

C. Vacation Rentals

For those who prefer a more private and home-like experience, vacation rentals can be a great option. Websites like Airbnb (https://www.airbnb.com/) and Booking.com (https://www.booking.com/) offer a variety of apartments and houses for rent in Belgrade, ranging from small studios to spacious family homes. Vacation rentals can be found in various neighborhoods across the city, allowing you to choose a location that suits your needs and preferences. Some popular neighborhoods for vacation rentals include the historic Stari Grad, the trendy Savamala district, and the more residential Dorćol.

D. Our recommended hotel: Hotel Moskva

Hotel Moskva is a historic hotel located in the heart of Belgrade, Serbia. Built-in 1908 in the neoclassical style, it's one of the city's most iconic landmarks. The hotel has been a symbol of Belgrade's glamour and luxury for over a century, hosting numerous famous guests such as Albert Einstein, Richard Nixon, and Indira Gandhi.

The hotel's interior is a mix of classic and modern design, creating a unique and elegant atmosphere. The rooms are spacious and comfortable, equipped with modern amenities such as free Wi-Fi, air conditioning, and a flat-screen TV. The hotel also features a restaurant, a cafe, a spa center, and a casino, making it a perfect place to stay for both leisure and business travelers.

One of the hotel's highlights is the Cafe Moskva, which is a popular meeting spot for locals and tourists alike. It has been serving delicious cakes and pastries since 1908 and is a must-visit for anyone with a sweet tooth. The Cafe Moskva's interior is decorated in the Art Nouveau style, with beautiful stained glass windows and a charming atmosphere.

26

Another highlight of the Hotel Moskva is its location. It's situated in the heart of the city, just a few minutes' walk from the Knez Mihailova pedestrian street, the Republic Square, and the National Theatre. The hotel is also well-connected to the city's public transportation system, making it easy to explore other parts of the city.

Overall, the Hotel Moskva is a perfect choice for those who want to experience the glamour and luxury of Belgrade's past while enjoying modern amenities and a convenient location.

Hotel Name: Moskva
Address: Terazije 20| **Tel**: +381 113642069|
http://www.hotelmoskva.rs/en| **Price**: About 120e 2 bed room
TripAdvisor: link| **Booking.com**: Click here to read reviews and book the hotel online

V. Sightseeing and Attractions

A. Historical Landmarks

Belgrade has a rich history that spans over two millennia, with numerous historical landmarks showcasing the city's diverse cultural influences. Two of the most iconic historical landmarks in Belgrade are Kalemegdan Fortress and St. Sava Temple.

1. Kalemegdan Fortress

Kalemegdan Fortress, also known as Belgrade Fortress, is the city's most famous landmark and an essential stop for any visitor. Perched atop a hill overlooking the confluence of the Sava and

Danube rivers, the fortress has a history dating back to the 3rd century BC. Throughout the centuries, it has been occupied and rebuilt by various empires, including the Romans, Byzantines, Ottomans, and Austrians.

Today, Kalemegdan Fortress is a large park and cultural complex that houses several attractions, including:

- *Military Museum:* Showcasing a vast collection of weapons, uniforms, and military equipment from different eras, the Military Museum is a must-see for history buffs.

- *Ruzica Church:* This unique church, with chandeliers made from spent bullet casings and swords, was once a gunpowder storage facility.

- *Victor Monument:* Erected in 1928, this iconic statue symbolizes victory and freedom and offers panoramic views of the city and the rivers below.

Entrance to the Kalemegdan Park is free, but some attractions within the fortress may charge a small admission fee. The fortress is open daily from 6:00 AM to midnight.

2. St. Sava Temple

St. Sava Temple, also known as the Church of Saint Sava, is one of the most recognizable landmarks in Belgrade and the largest Orthodox church in Serbia. The temple is dedicated to St. Sava, the founder of the Serbian Orthodox Church and a pivotal figure in Serbian history.

Construction of the temple began in 1935, but due to various challenges, including World War II and political turmoil, it was not completed until the 21st century. The impressive white marble building, with its massive central dome and four smaller domes, is an architectural masterpiece, combining elements of Serbian-Byzantine and Neo-Byzantine styles.

Visitors can explore the temple's vast interior, adorned with intricate mosaics, frescoes, and an impressive central chandelier. The crypt, located beneath the temple, houses a museum, a treasury, and various relics.

The St. Sava Temple is open daily from 7:00 AM to 7:00 PM, and admission is free. However, donations are encouraged to support the ongoing maintenance and decoration of the temple. When visiting, remember to dress modestly and be respectful, as the temple is an active place of worship.

Both Kalemegdan Fortress and St. Sava Temple offer unique insights into Belgrade's rich history and are must-visit attractions for anyone exploring the city.

B. Museums and Galleries

Belgrade is home to numerous museums and galleries that showcase the city's rich history, culture, and artistic heritage. Two notable museums worth visiting are the Nikola Tesla Museum and the Museum of Contemporary Art.

1. Nikola Tesla Museum

The Nikola Tesla Museum (https://nikolateslamuseum.org/) is dedicated to the life and work of the famous Serbian-American inventor, scientist, and engineer, Nikola Tesla. Tesla's pioneering work in the fields of electrical engineering and electromagnetism laid the foundation for modern electrical power systems and wireless communication technologies.

The museum, located in a residential area close to the city center, houses a vast collection of Tesla's personal belongings, documents, and original inventions. Among the most notable exhibits are:

- *Tesla's Ashes:* Tesla's ashes are housed in a golden sphere, a symbol of his global influence and impact.

- *Tesla Coil:* A working replica of the Tesla Coil, one of his most famous inventions, demonstrates the principles of wireless energy transmission.

- *Interactive Exhibits:* The museum features several interactive exhibits, allowing visitors to engage with and better understand Tesla's work.

Guided tours in English are available and included in the admission price, which is 500 RSD (about 4.3 EUR) for adults and 250 RSD (about 2.1 EUR) for children and students. The museum is open daily from 10:00 AM to 6:00 PM, except on Mondays.

2. Museum of Contemporary Art

The Museum of Contemporary Art (http://www.msub.org.rs/) is an essential stop for art lovers visiting Belgrade. Located in the New Belgrade district, near the confluence of the Sava and Danube rivers, the museum is housed in a modernist building designed by renowned architect Ivan Antić.

The museum's permanent collection features over 8,000 works, including paintings, sculptures, photographs, and multimedia installations by Serbian and international artists from the 20th and

21st centuries. Some of the most notable artists represented in the collection are Marina Abramović, Dušan Otašević, and Olja Ivanjicki.

In addition to its permanent collection, the Museum of Contemporary Art hosts temporary exhibitions, educational programs, and cultural events throughout the year.

The museum is open from 10:00 AM to 6:00 PM, Tuesday to Sunday, and closed on Mondays. The admission fee is 300 RSD (about 2.5 EUR) for adults, with reduced rates available for students, seniors, and groups.

Both the Nikola Tesla Museum and the Museum of Contemporary Art offer unique and engaging experiences for visitors interested in learning more about Belgrade's rich cultural heritage and the contributions of its most renowned citizens.

C. Parks and Outdoor Spaces

Belgrade offers several beautiful parks and outdoor spaces where visitors can enjoy nature, engage in recreational activities, or simply relax. Two popular outdoor destinations in the city are Ada Ciganlija and Košutnjak Park.

1. Ada Ciganlija

Ada Ciganlija (https://www.adaciganlija.rs/en), often referred to as Belgrade's "Sea," is a river island turned peninsula, located on the Sava River. It is a popular recreational area for both locals and tourists, offering various activities, including swimming, sunbathing, cycling, and picnicking.

During the summer months, the island's pebble beaches attract thousands of sunbathers, while the lake's clean and calm waters are perfect for swimming. For more adventurous visitors, Ada Ciganlija also offers several water sports facilities, such as kayaking, paddleboarding, and wakeboarding.

Cycling enthusiasts can enjoy the island's extensive network of bike paths, which connect to the city's broader cycling network. There are several bike rental shops on the island, with rental rates starting at around 300 RSD (about 2.5 EUR) per hour.

In addition to water sports and cycling, Ada Ciganlija features various sports facilities, including tennis courts, a golf course, and a skate park. There are also numerous cafés, bars, and restaurants, where visitors can enjoy a meal or drink while taking in the beautiful surroundings.

2. Košutnjak Park

Košutnjak Park (https://www.belgradestreets.com/2011/07/30/kosutnjak/) is a vast forested park located in the western part of Belgrade. Often referred to as the "lungs of Belgrade," the park covers an area of over 300 hectares, providing a peaceful retreat from the hustle and bustle of the city.

The park offers various recreational opportunities, including hiking, jogging, and cycling on its numerous trails, which vary in difficulty and length. One of the most popular trails leads to the highest point in the park, offering panoramic views of the city below.

Košutnjak Park is also home to several sports facilities, including a sports center with an indoor pool, tennis courts, and a soccer field. For families, the park features several playgrounds and picnic areas, making it an ideal destination for a day out with the kids.

Both Ada Ciganlija and Košutnjak Park offer beautiful outdoor spaces where visitors can unwind and enjoy nature while experiencing some of Belgrade's most popular recreational activities.

D. Unique Experiences

Belgrade offers several unique experiences that showcase the city's vibrant atmosphere and distinctive character. Two of these experiences are the Floating River Clubs (Splavovi) and the Zemun Quay.

1. Floating River Clubs (Splavovi)

Belgrade's Floating River Clubs, or Splavovi, are a unique and essential part of the city's nightlife scene. These floating venues, moored along the banks of the Sava and Danube rivers, offer a mix of bars, restaurants, and nightclubs. The Splavovi are particularly popular during the summer months, when their open-air decks provide the perfect setting for enjoying a drink or dancing the night away under the stars.

Each Splav has its unique atmosphere, with some focusing on electronic music, others on traditional Serbian turbo-folk, and some offering live bands or jazz performances. Popular Splavovi include:

- *Freestyler:* One of the most famous clubs in Belgrade, Freestyler (https://www.freestylerbelgrade.com/) offers a mix of electronic, house, and R&B music in a vibrant atmosphere.

- *20/44:* A more laid-back venue, 20/44 (https://www.facebook.com/Twenty-Forty-Four-2044-

164133473624494/) focuses on underground electronic music and alternative events, attracting a diverse crowd of music lovers.

- *Lasta:* Located on the Sava River, Lasta (https://lastaclub.com/) offers a sophisticated setting with a mix of electronic and house music, as well as themed events and guest DJs.

When visiting the Splavovi, it's essential to dress appropriately, as many venues have a strict dress code. Also, note that some clubs may charge a cover fee, especially on weekends or for special events.

2. Zemun Quay

Zemun Quay, located in the Zemun district along the Danube River, offers a unique experience of Belgrade's riverside charm. The quay is a popular destination for both locals and tourists, who come to enjoy its picturesque waterfront, lined with colorful buildings, lively cafés, and restaurants.

A leisurely stroll along the quay offers beautiful views of the river and the Great War Island, a nature reserve and bird sanctuary. Visitors can also rent bicycles or pedal boats, adding a fun and active element to their experience.

In addition to its scenic beauty, Zemun Quay is home to several historical landmarks, including the Gardos Tower, which offers panoramic views of the city, and the Church of St. Nicholas, a beautiful example of Serbian Orthodox architecture.

The Floating River Clubs (Splavovi) and Zemun Quay are two unique experiences that showcase Belgrade's vibrant atmosphere and distinctive charm, providing visitors with unforgettable memories of their time in the city.

VI. Food and Dining

A. Serbian Cuisine

Serbian cuisine is a delightful blend of Balkan, Mediterranean, and Ottoman influences, resulting in a rich and diverse culinary tradition. When dining in Belgrade, visitors should make sure to sample some of the traditional dishes and local drinks that the city has to offer.

1. Traditional Dishes

Some of the most popular traditional Serbian dishes include:

- *Ćevapi:* Grilled minced meat sausages, typically made from a mix of beef, pork, and lamb, served with flatbread, onions, and a side of kajmak (a creamy dairy spread).

- *Pljeskavica:* A spiced meat patty, similar to a burger, made from a mix of beef, pork, and lamb. It's often served with flatbread, onions, and various condiments, such as kajmak or ajvar (a red pepper and eggplant spread).

- *Sarma:* Rolled cabbage leaves stuffed with minced meat, rice, and spices, cooked in a tomato sauce. It's typically served as a main course with a side of mashed potatoes or bread.

- *Karadordeva šnicla:* A breaded and deep-fried meat roll stuffed with kajmak, named after the Serbian leader Karađorđe Petrović. This dish is often served with a side of mashed potatoes or French fries and a tartar sauce.

- *Gibanica:* A savory pastry made from layers of thin dough filled with a mixture of cheese, eggs, and sometimes spinach or meat.

To experience some of these traditional dishes, consider visiting one of Belgrade's many kafanas, which are traditional Serbian taverns. Some popular kafanas in the city include:

- *Question Mark (Znak Pitanja):* Located in a historic building near Kalemegdan Fortress, this is Belgrade's oldest kafana, dating back to 1823. The cozy atmosphere and traditional Serbian dishes make it a must-visit destination (Kralja Petra 6, 11000 Belgrade).

- *Tri šešira:* Situated in the lively Skadarlija district, Tri šešira has been serving traditional Serbian cuisine since 1864. The kafana often features live folk music, adding to the authentic dining experience (Skadarska 29, 11000 Belgrade).

2. Local Drinks

Serbia has a rich tradition of producing alcoholic beverages, and visitors should not miss the opportunity to sample some local drinks. Popular Serbian drinks include:

- *Rakija:* A strong fruit brandy, typically made from plums, but also produced with other fruits such as apricots, quinces, or grapes. Rakija is often served as an aperitif or digestif, and can be found in many flavors and varieties.

- *Wine:* Serbia has a long history of winemaking, with several wine regions producing quality wines, including reds, whites, and rosés. Some notable Serbian wines to try are Prokupac (a red wine grape variety) and Tamjanika (a white wine grape variety).

- *Beer:* Beer is a popular drink in Serbia, with both domestic and international brands widely available. Some local Serbian beers to try include Jelen, Lav, and Zaječarsko.

When exploring Belgrade's food and dining scene, be sure to indulge in the delicious and diverse flavors of traditional Serbian cuisine and local drinks. The city's many kafanas, restaurants, and bars offer an authentic taste of Serbia's rich culinary heritage.

B. Restaurants and Cafes

Belgrade's thriving food scene offers a wide range of dining options, from upscale fine dining establishments to local eateries and street food vendors. Visitors can experience the city's culinary diversity by exploring its various restaurants and cafes.

1. Fine Dining

Belgrade is home to several fine dining establishments, where visitors can enjoy a luxurious dining experience and sample exquisite international and Serbian cuisine. Some notable fine dining restaurants in the city include:

- *Dijagonala:* A contemporary restaurant offering a fusion of Serbian and international dishes, Dijagonala is known for its creative menu and stylish atmosphere. The restaurant also features an extensive wine list, showcasing both local and international selections (Dalmatinska 78, 11000 Belgrade; https://www.dijagonala.rs/).

- *Ambar:* Located in the trendy Beton Hala waterfront area, Ambar offers a modern interpretation of traditional Serbian and Balkan cuisine. The restaurant is famous for its innovative small plates and tasting menus, allowing diners to sample a wide variety of flavors (Karadjordjeva 2-4, 11000 Belgrade; https://www.ambarrestaurant.com/en/).

2. Local Eateries

For a more casual dining experience, visitors can explore Belgrade's many local eateries, which serve a variety of traditional Serbian and international dishes at affordable prices. Some popular local eateries include:

- *Buregdzinica Sarajevo:* This small, unassuming eatery is famous for its delicious and authentic Bosnian-style burek, a flaky pastry filled with cheese, meat, or spinach. Buregdzinica Sarajevo is the perfect spot for a quick, satisfying meal or snack (Gavrila Principa 44, 11000 Belgrade).

- *Bucko:* A popular pizzeria among locals, Bucko serves delicious thin-crust pizza by the slice, with a variety of toppings to choose from. The pizzeria also offers several vegan and vegetarian options (Požeška 118a, 11000 Belgrade; https://www.pizzabucko.rs/).

3. Street Food and Fast Food

Belgrade's street food scene offers a diverse range of options, from traditional Serbian fast food to international favorites. Some popular street food and fast food choices include:

- *Rostiljnica Marjan:* This popular grill is known for its tasty and affordable pljeskavica, ćevapi, and other grilled meat dishes. With generous portions and a casual, friendly atmosphere,

Rostiljnica Marjan is a must-visit spot for meat lovers (Vidikovački Venac 79, 11000 Belgrade).

- *Walter:* For a taste of Serbia's iconic ćevapi, head to Walter, a local chain with several locations throughout the city. Walter's ćevapi are served with fresh flatbread, onions, and a side of kajmak, offering a delicious and filling meal on the go (Bulevar Arsenija Čarnojevića 69, 11070 Belgrade; https://www.waltercevap.rs/).

Whether you're looking for a fine dining experience, a casual local eatery, or a quick street food snack, Belgrade offers a diverse array of dining options that cater to every taste and budget.

C. Vegetarian and Vegan Options

Belgrade has become increasingly accommodating to vegetarian and vegan diets, with a growing number of restaurants offering plant-based options. Here are some of the best vegetarian and vegan-friendly spots in the city:

1. *Radost Fina Kuhinjica:* This cozy, welcoming restaurant offers a diverse menu of vegetarian and vegan dishes, including soups, salads, main courses, and desserts. Their creative dishes often feature local and seasonal ingredients, and their menu includes gluten-free options as well (Pariska 3, 11000 Belgrade; https://www.radostfinakuhinjica.com/).

2. *Supermarket Deli:* Located in the trendy Dorćol district, Supermarket Deli offers a selection of vegetarian and vegan-friendly dishes, including sandwiches, salads, and smoothie bowls. The stylish atmosphere and friendly staff make it an excellent choice for a casual meal or coffee break (Strahinjića Bana 75, 11000 Belgrade; https://www.supermarket.rs/deli/).

3. *Moon Sushi Bar:* While not strictly a vegetarian or vegan restaurant, Moon Sushi Bar offers a range of plant-based sushi rolls and other dishes, making it a suitable choice for those looking for a more upscale dining experience with vegetarian or vegan options (Bulevar Mihajla Pupina 165, 11070 Belgrade; https://www.moonsushibar.rs/).

4. *Mayka:* This modern restaurant focuses on plant-based cuisine, offering a variety of vegan and vegetarian dishes inspired by both Serbian and international flavors. The menu includes a selection of salads, soups, main courses, and desserts, with many gluten-free options available (Kralja Petra 8, 11000 Belgrade; https://www.mayka.rs/).

5. *FitBar:* A health-focused eatery with several locations in Belgrade, FitBar offers a range of vegetarian and vegan options, including salads, wraps, and smoothies. Their menu emphasizes fresh, nutrient-dense ingredients, making it an excellent choice for a healthy meal or snack on the go (Nikole Pašića 26, 11000 Belgrade; https://www.fitbar.rs/).

With the growing number of vegetarian and vegan-friendly restaurants in Belgrade, visitors can easily find delicious plant-based options that cater to their dietary preferences.

VII. Nightlife and Entertainment

A. Clubs and Bars

Belgrade is known for its vibrant nightlife scene, with a wide range of clubs, bars, and entertainment venues catering to diverse tastes and preferences. Two popular areas for experiencing Belgrade's nightlife are the Splavovi, or floating river clubs, and the Savamala District.

1. Splavovi

As mentioned earlier, the Splavovi are a unique and essential part of Belgrade's nightlife scene. These floating venues, moored along the banks of the Sava and Danube rivers, offer a mix of bars, restaurants, and nightclubs. The Splavovi are particularly popular during the summer months when their open-air decks provide the perfect setting for enjoying a drink or dancing the night away under the stars.

Some popular Splavovi include:

- *Freestyler:* One of the most famous clubs in Belgrade, Freestyler (https://www.freestylerbelgrade.com/) offers a mix of electronic, house, and R&B music in a vibrant atmosphere.

- *20/44:* A more laid-back venue, 20/44 (https://www.facebook.com/Twenty-Forty-Four-2044-164133473624494/) focuses on underground electronic music and alternative events, attracting a diverse crowd of music lovers.

- *Lasta:* Located on the Sava River, Lasta (https://lastaclub.com/) offers a sophisticated setting with a mix of electronic and house music, as well as themed events and guest DJs.

2. Savamala District

The Savamala District, located near the Sava River, is another popular area for nightlife in Belgrade. This revitalized neighborhood is home to a mix of clubs, bars, and cultural venues, making it an ideal destination for a night out on the town.

Some notable clubs and bars in the Savamala District include:

- *Mikser House:* A multifunctional space that hosts concerts, parties, and various cultural events, Mikser House (https://www.mikser.rs/) is a hub of creativity and entertainment in Savamala.

- *KC Grad:* This cultural center and club (https://www.gradbeograd.eu/) hosts a variety of events, including live music, DJ sets, and art exhibitions, attracting a diverse and artistic crowd.

- *Ben Akiba:* A comedy club and bar with a laid-back atmosphere, Ben Akiba (https://www.facebook.com/ben.akiba.comedy.club/) offers a mix of comedy shows, live music, and DJ sets, making it a popular destination for a fun and relaxed night out.

When exploring Belgrade's nightlife scene, be sure to check out the unique atmosphere of the Splavovi and the diverse entertainment options in the Savamala District. These two popular areas offer a wide range of clubs, bars, and venues, ensuring that visitors can find the perfect spot for a memorable night out in the city.

B. Live Music Venues

Belgrade is home to a thriving live music scene, with venues hosting local and international acts spanning various genres, from rock and jazz to traditional Serbian music. Some notable live music venues in the city include:

1. *Dom omladine Beograda (Belgrade Youth Center):* This cultural center (https://www.domomladine.org/) hosts a variety of events, including live music concerts, art exhibitions, and workshops. The venue has a diverse program, featuring both local and international acts across various genres.

2. *BitefArtCafe:* Located in the heart of Belgrade, BitefArtCafe (https://www.bitefartcafe.rs/) is a stylish venue that hosts live music performances, DJ sets, and other cultural events. The venue's program includes local and international artists, with a focus on jazz, soul, and world music.

3. *Klub Gun:* This intimate live music venue (https://www.facebook.com/klub.gun/) is located in the Dorćol district and hosts a range of local and international acts, including rock, blues, and alternative music.

C. Cultural Events and Festivals

Belgrade hosts numerous cultural events and festivals throughout the year, showcasing the city's rich artistic and creative scene. Some of the most notable events and festivals include:

1. *Belgrade Beer Fest:* Held annually in August at Ušće Park, the Belgrade Beer Fest (https://www.belgradebeerfest.com/) is one of the largest beer festivals in Southeast Europe, featuring over

450 different beer brands, live music performances, and various entertainment activities.

2. *Belgrade International Documentary Film Festival:* This annual festival (https://beldocs.rs/) takes place in May and showcases a selection of documentary films from around the world, including screenings, panel discussions, and workshops.

3. *Belgrade Jazz Festival:* Held in October, the Belgrade Jazz Festival (https://www.belgradejazzfest.rs/) features local and international jazz artists performing at various venues across the city. The festival includes concerts, workshops, and jam sessions, attracting jazz enthusiasts from around the world.

4. *EXIT Festival:* Although not held in Belgrade, EXIT Festival (https://www.exitfest.org/) is one of the largest music festivals in the region, taking place in Novi Sad, just a short drive from Belgrade. The festival features a diverse lineup of international and local acts, spanning various genres, including rock, electronic, and world music.

When visiting Belgrade, be sure to explore the city's live music venues and take part in its numerous cultural events and festivals to fully experience the vibrant atmosphere and creativity that the city has to offer.

VIII. Shopping in Belgrade

Belgrade offers a diverse shopping experience, with options ranging from modern shopping malls to traditional local markets and unique specialty shops. Whether you're looking for international brands, local products, or memorable souvenirs, Belgrade has something to offer every shopper.

A. Shopping Malls

Belgrade is home to several shopping malls, where visitors can find a mix of international and local brands, as well as various dining and entertainment options. Some of the most popular shopping malls in the city include:

1. *Ušće Shopping Center:* Located at the confluence of the Sava and Danube rivers, Ušće Shopping Center (https://www.usceshoppingcenter.com/) is the largest mall in Belgrade, featuring over 150 stores, a multiplex cinema, and a variety of dining options.

2. *Delta City:* Situated in the New Belgrade district, Delta City (https://www.deltacity.rs/) is another popular shopping destination, offering a mix of fashion, electronics, and home goods stores, as well as a cinema and numerous dining choices.

B. Local Markets

For a more authentic shopping experience, visitors can explore Belgrade's local markets, which offer a wide range of fresh produce, handmade crafts, and other products. Some notable markets in the city include:

1. *Zeleni Venac Market:* One of the oldest and most famous markets in Belgrade, Zeleni Venac Market is located near the

city center and offers a variety of fresh fruits, vegetables, and other local products.

2. *Bajloni Market:* Also known as Skadarlija Market, Bajloni Market is situated in the historic Skadarlija district and features a mix of produce, meat, and dairy products, as well as local handicrafts and souvenirs.

C. Souvenir and Specialty Shops

When looking for unique souvenirs or specialty items, Belgrade offers a variety of shops where visitors can find traditional Serbian crafts, local products, and other memorable gifts. Some popular souvenir and specialty shops in the city include:

1. *Serbian Heritage:* This specialty store (https://www.serbianheritage.rs/) offers a selection of high-quality traditional Serbian handicrafts, including ceramics, textiles, and wooden items. Located in the Knez Mihailova shopping area, Serbian Heritage is an excellent place to find unique and authentic souvenirs.

2. *Zlatara Majdanpek:* A renowned Serbian jewelry brand, Zlatara Majdanpek (https://www.zlataramajdanpek.rs/) offers a range of gold and silver jewelry inspired by traditional Serbian designs. With several locations throughout the city, Zlatara Majdanpek is a popular choice for those looking for a special gift or keepsake.

IX. Practical Information

A. Currency and Payments

The official currency in Serbia is the Serbian Dinar (RSD). It is advisable to have local currency on hand, as many small businesses and street vendors may not accept other currencies or credit cards. There are numerous exchange offices (menjačnica) throughout the city, as well as ATMs where you can withdraw cash. Major credit cards are widely accepted in hotels, restaurants, and larger stores, but it's always a good idea to carry some cash for smaller purchases and tips.

B. Safety Tips

Belgrade is generally considered a safe city for tourists, but like any urban area, it's essential to take basic safety precautions:

1. Keep your belongings secure and avoid displaying valuable items, such as expensive jewelry or electronics, in crowded or unfamiliar areas.

2. Be aware of your surroundings and avoid poorly lit or deserted streets, especially late at night.

3. Use official taxis or ride-sharing apps to ensure a safe and reliable ride.

4. If you need assistance, don't hesitate to ask locals or the staff at your accommodation for help or advice.

C. Health and Medical Facilities

Belgrade has a number of public and private healthcare facilities, with many doctors and medical professionals able to communicate in English. In case of a medical emergency, dial 194 for an ambulance. It is advisable to have travel insurance that covers medical expenses, as well as any necessary prescriptions or vaccinations before traveling.

Some notable hospitals and clinics in Belgrade include:

1. *Belgrade Clinical Center:* A large public hospital offering a wide range of medical services (Pasterova 2, 11000 Belgrade; http://www.kcs.ac.rs/).

2. *Bel Medic:* A private medical facility with a variety of specialties, including emergency care (Koste Jovanovića 87, 11000 Belgrade; https://www.belmedic.rs/).

D. Language and Communication

The official language in Belgrade is Serbian, which is written in both Cyrillic and Latin scripts. While many locals, especially younger generations, speak English or other European languages, it is always appreciated when visitors make an effort to learn a few basic Serbian phrases. Some helpful words and phrases include:

1. Dobar dan (Good day)

2. Hvala (Thank you)

3. Izvinite (Excuse me)

4. Molim (Please)

5. Govorite li engleski? (Do you speak English?)

In general, Belgraders are friendly and welcoming, and they will be more than happy to help you with directions, recommendations, or other assistance if you approach them politely and with respect.

X. Day Trips from Belgrade

A. Novi Sad

Novi Sad, the second-largest city in Serbia, is an excellent day trip destination from Belgrade. Located about 90 km north of the capital, Novi Sad offers a rich history, charming architecture, and a vibrant cultural scene. Here is a suggested hour-by-hour itinerary for a day trip to Novi Sad, complete with activities, information, prices, websites, and tips:

8:00 AM - Departure from Belgrade

Start your day early by catching a bus or train from Belgrade to Novi Sad. The journey takes approximately 1.5 to 2 hours. Tickets can be purchased at the station or online at https://www.bas.rs/ or https://www.srbvoz.rs/eng/. Bus tickets cost around 600-800 RSD, while train tickets are typically 360-540 RSD.

10:00 AM - Arrival in Novi Sad

Upon arriving at the Novi Sad bus or train station, make your way to the city center. You can walk (about 20 minutes), take a taxi, or use a local bus (https://www.gspns.rs/en).

10:30 AM - Explore the Old Town

Begin your day in Novi Sad by exploring the Old Town, known as Stari Grad. Stroll along the pedestrian zone, Zmaj Jovina Street, and

Dunavska Street, where you'll find numerous shops, cafes, and historical buildings. Don't miss the picturesque square, Trg Slobode, with the City Hall and Name of Mary Church.

12:00 PM - Visit the Museum of Vojvodina

Discover the region's rich history at the Museum of Vojvodina (https://www.muzejvojvodine.org.rs/index.php/en/), which showcases a vast collection of artifacts, ranging from prehistoric times to the present. The entrance fee is 200 RSD for adults, and 100 RSD for students and seniors.

1:30 PM - Lunch at Project 72 Wine & Deli

Enjoy a delicious lunch at Project 72 Wine & Deli (https://project72.rs/), a trendy restaurant in the city center offering a variety of dishes, including Serbian cuisine, as well as an extensive wine list. Expect to spend around 1000-1500 RSD per person for a meal and drink.

3:00 PM - Visit the Petrovaradin Fortress

After lunch, head to the Petrovaradin Fortress, an iconic symbol of Novi Sad. Cross the Varadin Bridge and follow the signs up to the fortress. Explore the grounds, visit the museum, and take in the stunning views of the city and Danube River. There is no entrance fee for the fortress grounds, but the City Museum of Novi Sad (https://www.mpg.rs/) inside the fortress charges 200 RSD for adults and 100 RSD for students and seniors.

5:00 PM - Walk along the Danube Promenade

Descend from the fortress and enjoy a relaxing walk along the Danube Promenade (Kej). This scenic riverside area is lined with cafes and bars, making it a perfect spot for a coffee or early evening drink.

7:00 PM - Dinner at Fish & Zeleniš

For dinner, try Fish & Zeleniš (https://www.fishzelenis.rs/), a popular restaurant near the promenade that specializes in fish and seafood dishes, as well as a selection of salads and vegetarian options. Expect to spend around 1500-2000 RSD per person for a meal and drink.

9:00 PM - Return to Belgrade

After dinner, make your way back to the Novi Sad bus or train station to catch your return transport to Belgrade. As the last buses and trains usually depart between 9:00 PM and 10:00 PM, be sure to check the schedules in advance and allow sufficient time to reach the station. Tickets can be purchased at the station or online at https://www.bas.rs/ or https://www.srbvoz.rs/eng/.

11:00 PM - Arrival in Belgrade

Arrive back in Belgrade after an exciting day of exploring Novi Sad. With a memorable day trip under your belt, you'll have experienced the charm and history of one of Serbia's most vibrant cities.

Tips for your day trip to Novi Sad:

1. Wear comfortable shoes, as you'll be doing a lot of walking throughout the day.

2. Bring a hat, sunscreen, and a reusable water bottle to stay hydrated and protected from the sun.

3. Keep an eye on your belongings, especially in crowded areas and on public transportation.

4. Consider hiring a local guide for a personalized tour of the city. Websites like ToursByLocals (https://www.toursbylocals.com/) or GetYourGuide (https://www.getyourguide.com/) offer various guided tour options.

5. Don't forget your camera, as Novi Sad is full of beautiful and photogenic spots!

B. Sremski Karlovci

Sremski Karlovci is a picturesque town in the Vojvodina region of Serbia, known for its rich history, stunning architecture, and wine production. Located about 57 km north of Belgrade, it makes for a perfect day trip. Here's a suggested hour-by-hour itinerary for a day trip to Sremski Karlovci, complete with activities, information, prices, websites, and tips:

9:00 AM - Departure from Belgrade

Begin your day by catching a bus or train from Belgrade to Sremski Karlovci. The journey takes approximately 1 to 1.5 hours. Tickets can be purchased at the station or online at https://www.bas.rs/ or https://www.srbvoz.rs/eng/. Bus tickets cost around 500-600 RSD, while train tickets are typically 300-400 RSD.

10:30 AM - Arrival in Sremski Karlovci

Upon arrival at the Sremski Karlovci bus or train station, make your way to the town center. You can walk (about 15 minutes), take a taxi, or use a local bus (https://www.gspns.rs/en).

11:00 AM - Explore the Town Center

Start your day in Sremski Karlovci by exploring the charming town center. Stroll through the main square, Trg Branka Radičevića, and admire the beautiful Baroque architecture, including the St. Nicholas Cathedral, the Karlovci Grammar School, and the Patriarch's Residence.

12:00 PM - Visit the Chapel of Peace

Head to the Chapel of Peace (https://www.turizamkarlovci.rs/en/), a historic site where the Treaty of Karlowitz was signed in 1699. This small, octagonal building is a symbol of the town's historical importance. Entrance fee is 150 RSD for adults, and 100 RSD for students and seniors.

1:00 PM - Lunch at Pod Lozom

Enjoy a traditional Serbian lunch at Pod Lozom (https://podlozom.rs/), a popular restaurant in the town center. Sample local dishes like fish paprikash or stuffed peppers, and taste some of the region's famous wines. Expect to spend around 1000-1500 RSD per person for a meal and drink.

3:00 PM - Wine Tasting at a Local Winery

Sremski Karlovci is renowned for its wine production, so a visit to a local winery is a must. Some popular options include the Živanović Winery (http://www.vinarija-zivanovic.com/) and the Kovačević Winery (https://www.vinarijakovacevic.rs/en/). Enjoy a guided tour of the winery, followed by a tasting of their finest wines. Prices vary, but expect to spend around 1000-1500 RSD per person for a tour and tasting.

5:00 PM - Walk along the Danube River

After the wine tasting, take a leisurely walk along the Danube River and enjoy the scenic views. You can also visit the nearby Strand beach, a popular spot for swimming and sunbathing during the summer months.

7:00 PM - Dinner at Tri Fenjera

For dinner, try Tri Fenjera (http://trifenjera.rs/), a cozy restaurant offering a variety of traditional Serbian dishes and local wines. Expect to spend around 1000-1500 RSD per person for a meal and drink.

9:00 PM - Return to Belgrade

After dinner, make your way back to the Sremski Karlovci bus or train station to catch your return transport to Belgrade. As the last buses and trains usually depart between 9:00 PM and 10:00 PM, be sure to check the schedules in advance and allow sufficient time to reach the station. Tickets can be purchased at the station or online at https://www.bas.rs/ or https://www.srbvoz.rs/eng/.

11:00 PM - Arrival in Belgrade

Arrive back in Belgrade after a memorable day of exploring the historic town of Sremski Karlovci. You'll have tasted some of the region's finest wines, learned about its rich history, and enjoyed some traditional Serbian cuisine.

C. Avala Mountain

Avala Mountain is a popular day trip destination from Belgrade, located just 16 km south of the city center. It offers stunning views, fresh air, and numerous outdoor activities. Here's a suggested hour-by-hour itinerary for a day trip to Avala Mountain, complete with activities, information, prices, websites, and tips:

9:00 AM - Departure from Belgrade

Start your day by taking a taxi or bus from Belgrade to Avala Mountain. The journey takes approximately 30-40 minutes by taxi or 45 minutes by bus. Bus number 400 runs from the Slavija Square to Avala every hour (https://www.gsp.rs/).

10:00 AM - Arrival at Avala Tower

Upon arriving at Avala Mountain, head to the Avala Tower (https://www.avalskitoranj.rs/), the tallest structure in Serbia, standing at 205 meters tall. Take the elevator to the observation deck at the top and enjoy panoramic views of the surrounding area. Entrance fee is 500 RSD for adults and 250 RSD for children.

11:00 AM - Hiking in Avala Forest

Avala Mountain is home to a vast forest with numerous hiking trails. Take a leisurely stroll or more challenging hike through the forest and enjoy the fresh air and peaceful nature. You can also rent a bike to explore the mountain (https://www.avalski-bike.rs/).

1:00 PM - Lunch at Vrelo Restaurant

After a morning of exploring, head to Vrelo Restaurant (https://www.vrelomeravan.rs/restoran/), located at the foot of the mountain, for a traditional Serbian lunch. Try the cevapi or grilled meat dishes, and don't forget to sample the local Rakija (brandy). Expect to spend around 1000-1500 RSD per person for a meal and drink.

3:00 PM - Visit the Monument to the Unknown Hero

The Monument to the Unknown Hero
(https://www.turistickikanal.net/en/monument-to-the-unknown-hero/) is a symbol of Serbian bravery and sacrifice during World War I. The monument is located at the top of Avala Mountain and is accessible by car or on foot. Entrance to the monument is free.

5:00 PM - Visit the Avala Film Park

Avala Film Park (http://www.avlafilmpark.rs/en/) is a unique open-air film studio located at the foot of Avala Mountain. Take a guided tour of the studio, learn about Serbian film history, and see where famous movies and TV shows were filmed. The entrance fee for the tour is 400 RSD for adults and 200 RSD for children.

7:00 PM - Dinner at Stara Hercegovina

For dinner, try Stara Hercegovina (https://www.starahercegovina.com/), a traditional Serbian restaurant located in the city center of Belgrade. The menu offers various meat dishes and Balkan specialties, and the atmosphere is cozy and authentic. Expect to spend around 1000-1500 RSD per person for a meal and drink.

9:00 PM - Return to Belgrade

After dinner, take a taxi or bus back to Belgrade, feeling refreshed and rejuvenated after a day in nature.

Our 3-Day Travel Itinerary to Belgrade

Day 1 in Belgrade: Arrival, Walk and Monuments

11.00 - Arrival at Belgrade Nikola Tesla Airport

As you arrive at the Belgrade Nikola Tesla Airport, which is located approximately 18 km away from the city center, it's time to start your adventure in Belgrade.

11.30 - Pass through passport control and get luggage

Pass through passport control, which usually takes around 30 minutes, and collect your luggage.

11.35 - Transportation from the Airport to the Hotel

Take a taxi outside the airport. There are various taxi associations with fixed prices per km ride, and it's irrelevant which one you choose. Expect to pay around 10-12 euros for a ride from the airport to the Hotel Moskva.

12.00 - Check in to the Moskva Hotel and Walk to Kalemegdan

Check in to the Moskva Hotel, which is a historic hotel located in the city center, and begin your tour with a pleasant walk to Kalemegdan. It's only a 20-minute walk from the hotel to Kalemegdan, which is a vast park and fortress complex in the heart of Belgrade. Explore the Belgrade Fortress, the statue of the Winner, and the fountain of Mehmed Pasa Sokolovic. Climb the hill and enjoy the stunning view of the Sava and Danube rivers. Take some time to stroll around and enjoy the park's beauty.

15.00 - Lunch at Gradska Restaurant

Go for a 10-minute walk to the Gradska Restaurant, which is located at Visokog Stevana 43a (Mike Alasa 54). This restaurant serves traditional Serbian cuisine, and the lamb specialties are a must-try. Expect to spend around 6 to 12 euros per meal.

16.30 - Visit the Gardos Tower

Gardos is one of the oldest neighborhoods in Belgrade, and the Gardos Tower is the only Austro-Hungarian watchtower that has remained in other countries. At that time, Zemun was still part of the Austro-Hungarian Empire. The tower dates back to the end of the 19th century. Gardos is also the place where you can follow population continuity from Neolithic to the present day. At the 2nd floor of Kula Gardos, you will find a great viewpoint from where you can see the four parts of the world. See the remains of the old Zemun Fortress behind the tower, dating back to the 14th century. The entrance fee to Gardos Tower is 150 RSD. To get here, take bus line no.16 at Bulevar Despota Stefana. Exit at Goce Delceva station and walk to Kula Gardos.

19.00 - Dinner at Restaurant Saran

For dinner, head to Restaurant Saran, which is located at Kej Oslobođenja 53. This restaurant is known for its fish specialties, and the prices range from 9 to 12 euros per meal.

20.00 - Sava and Danube Cruise

Take a boat sightseeing tour of Belgrade, which lasts about 2 hours. Enjoy the panorama of Zemun, Gardos Tower, Tower Nebojsa, Ruzica Church, Kalemegdan, Belgrade bridges, and all other monuments that can be seen on foot. The Sava and Danube Cruise can be booked through the Klub Kej website or by calling +381 64 825 11 20. The cost is 400 RSD per ticket.

22.00 - Return to the Hotel

After the cruise, return to the hotel to relax and have a good rest for the next day. To get back to the hotel, take bus line no.15 at SIV station and exit at Zeleni Venac station. The ride takes around 15 minutes.

Day 1 in Belgrade is a great introduction to the city's rich history and beautiful landmarks. You get to explore the Belgrade Fortress, enjoy a stunning view of the Sava and Danube rivers, taste traditional Serbian cuisine, and experience a boat sightseeing tour of the city. The itinerary is easy to follow and includes specific information on transportation, addresses, and costs, making your visit stress-free and enjoyable. Don't forget to take plenty of pictures and make unforgettable memories in the beautiful city of Belgrade.

Day 1 in Belgrade Map

Below you can see the Map with the suggested activities for your first day in Belgrade. This map is accessible online in a Google Maps format, which will help you to navigate easily on foot, on bus, tram and car, when you are in the city.

You can get it at: <u>Click Here to Get this Map on Google Maps</u>

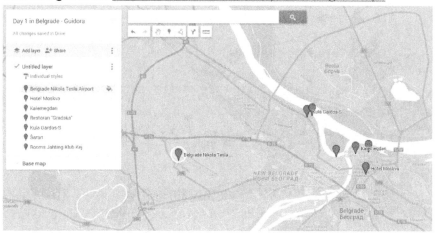

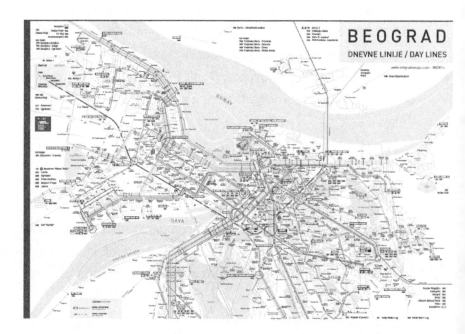

<u>You can see the map of public transport here</u>.

Or you can ask a passenger how to get from point A to point B. People are very friendly and proficient with English.

National Museum of Art

Entrance: 200RSD
Working hours: see the complete timetable

The National Museum is the oldest museum institution in Serbia. It is established in 1844. The most valuable exhibition is the Miroslav's Gospel, the oldest Cyrillic document that exists, which holds a beautiful and rich decoration. Learn parts of the history of the Balkan region from the 7th millennial BC to the 20th century. See the works of some great Serbian artists such as Nadezda Petrovic, Sava Sumanovic, Paja Jovanovic, Ivan Mestrovic, Milena Pavlovic Baril. See the great collection of foreign painters including Mondrian, Matisse, Monet, Kandinsky and Chagall.

Kula Gardos

Entrance: 150RSD
Working hours: 11am-8pm

Kula Gardos dates back since 1896 and it is one of the 4 Millennium that Austro-Hungarian Empire built on the four parts of the world in the farthest cities in its Empire. At that time, Zemun was still part of the Austro-Hungary, while Belgrade was part of the Serbian kingdom. Kula Gardos was built on the fundaments of the ancient Zemun's fortress Taurunum. There is a permament exhibition dedicated to the Serbian's famous scientist *Milutin Milankovic*. When you climb to the second floor, you will find a great viewpoint, from where you can enjoy an amazing view to Danube, Zemun and Belgrade.

Don't let the name trick you: this tower is also called *Millennium Tower* or Tower of *Sibnjanin Janko*

White Palace and King's Palace

Entrance: 450RSD
Working hours: Mon-Fri 9am-9pm, Sat 9am-5pm, Sun 10am-4pm
White Palace is a former royal residence of the *Karađorđević* dynasty. The White Palace is located in the same complex as the Royal Palace, the official residence of the Karađorđević royal family. The Palaces are surrounded by the beautiful flowered parks. Inside the Palaces there is a great art collection, from artists like Poussin, Rembrandt, Rubens and famous Yugoslavian artists including Ivan Mestrovic, Paja Jovanovic, Djura Jaksic.

The Temple of Saint Sava

Entrance: free of charge

Church of Saint Sava (often referred to as temple) is located on the Vračar plateau in Belgrade and it's one of the largest Orthodox churches in the world. Saint Sava was the founder of the Serbian Orthodox Church. The Temple is built on the location where his remains were burned in 1595 by the Turks. The building of the church is strictly financed by donations. Throughout the years, this church has become the symbol of the Serbian religious faith.

Nikola Tesla Museum

Entrance: 500RSD

Working hours: Tue-Sun 10am-6pm, Mon closed

The material for the Museum arrived in Belgrade according to the decision of the American court, which declared Mr. Sava Kosanovic, Tesla's nephew, as the only rightful heir; in accordance with Tesla's last wish, Mr. Kosanovic transferred all the documents and Tesla's personal things in Belgrade. It is the only museum in the world which preserves the personal inheritance of Nikola Tesla. Tesla was a supreme scientist whose patents include the design of the modern alternating current (AC) electricity supply system, among many others.

Who is Nikola Tesla

Nikola Tesla was a Serbian-American inventor, electrical engineer, mechanical engineer, and futurist who is best known for his contributions to the design of the modern alternating current (AC) electricity supply system. He was born on July 10, 1856, in Smiljan, Croatia, which was then part of the Austrian Empire. He passed away on January 7, 1943, in New York City, United States.

Tesla's early life was marked by academic achievement, and he was a gifted student who excelled in mathematics and science. He began his studies in electrical engineering at the Austrian Polytechnic in Graz, Austria, before moving to Prague, Czech Republic, to attend Charles-Ferdinand University. In 1884, he moved to the United States, where he worked as an assistant to Thomas Edison.

Tesla's most significant contributions to science and technology came in the form of his inventions and discoveries in the field of electrical engineering. His work on the design and implementation of AC electrical systems is perhaps his most significant achievement. This work led to the development of the AC generator, which became the standard for electricity distribution across the world.

Tesla also worked on other significant inventions during his career. He developed the Tesla coil, a type of transformer circuit used to produce high-voltage, low-current, high-frequency alternating-current electricity. The Tesla coil has been used in numerous applications, including radio communications, television sets, and even medical equipment.

Another invention for which Tesla is known is the Tesla turbine, a bladeless turbine that uses boundary-layer effects to convert fluid flow into rotational motion. Tesla envisioned the turbine as a potential replacement for traditional steam turbines, and although his design never saw widespread use, it remains an influential invention in the field of fluid mechanics.

Tesla's contributions to science and technology have earned him numerous accolades and honors. He was inducted into the National Inventors Hall of Fame in 1975, and in 1983 the United States Congress declared his birthday, July 10, as "Nikola Tesla Day." He is also the subject of numerous books, films, and television shows, and his legacy continues to inspire scientists and engineers to this day.

In Belgrade, visitors can visit the Nikola Tesla Museum, which was established in 1952 to preserve Tesla's legacy and his personal belongings. The museum contains numerous exhibits showcasing Tesla's inventions, documents, and personal effects, including a replica of his famous Tesla coil. The museum is located in the central part of the city, and visitors can easily reach it by public transportation or taxi. It's a must-visit for anyone interested in the life and work of one of the world's greatest inventors.

The Residence of Knjeginja Ljubica

Entrance: Free of charge
Working hours: Tue, Wed, Fri, 10am-5pm, Thu 10am-6pm, Sat 12pm-8pm, Mon closed

The Residence of Princess Ljubica is one of the few buildings surviving from the first reign of Prince Miloš Obrenović. The residence, that was built from 1829 to 1831, was intended to become a luxurious court of the Serbian ruling dynasty, i.e. the Obrenovićs. In accordance with its historical, artistic and heritage value, the Belgrade authorities decided to repurpose it as a museum. The exhibition includes a representative selection of fine and applied art objects, that belonged to the members of the ruling (Obrenović) dynasty and to other prominent bourgeois families.

Memorial Museum of Ivo Andric

Entrance: Free of charge
Working hours: Thu, Wed, Fri, Sat 10am-6pm, Thu 12pm-8pm, Sun 10am-2pm, Mon closed

Ivo Andric is one of the most significant Serbian figures of all time; he is the only Nobel Prize laureate from Serbia, winning the laureate for his contribution to the literature. After his death, the apartment where he lived during his years in Belgrade, was turned into a Memorial museum dedicated to him. The exhibition includes photos, documents and personal artifacts and medals.

Who is Ivo Andric

Ivo Andrić was a Bosnian-Serbian writer and diplomat who is considered one of the greatest literary figures of the 20th century. He was born on October 9, 1892, in Dolac, Bosnia and Herzegovina, which was then part of the Austro-Hungarian Empire. He passed away on March 13, 1975, in Belgrade, Serbia.

Andrić's early life was marked by political and social upheaval in the Balkans, and he witnessed firsthand the effects of ethnic and religious tensions that would come to define the region. He studied philosophy and literature in Zagreb, Croatia, before moving to Vienna, Austria, to continue his studies.

Andrić's literary career began in the 1920s, and he published numerous works of poetry, fiction, and non-fiction over the course of his lifetime. His most significant works include the novel "The Bridge on the Drina," which won the Nobel Prize for Literature in 1961, and the collection of short stories "Ex Ponto."

Andrić's writing is known for its exploration of the complex history and culture of the Balkans. His works often explore themes of identity, memory, and the legacy of conflict, and his writing is characterized by a lyrical style and an attention to detail.

In addition to his literary career, Andrić was also a diplomat, serving as Yugoslavia's ambassador to Germany and other countries during the 1940s and 1950s. He was a vocal opponent of the Nazi regime and worked to promote the interests of Yugoslavia on the international stage.

In Belgrade, visitors can visit the Ivo Andrić Museum, which is dedicated to the writer's life and work. The museum is located in Andrić's former home in the Old Town neighborhood of Belgrade and contains numerous exhibits showcasing his personal belongings, manuscripts, and other artifacts. Visitors can also explore the nearby Andrićev Venac, a pedestrian street named in his honor that is lined with bookstores, cafes, and other cultural attractions.

Andrić's legacy continues to inspire writers and readers around the world, and his works remain a testament to the power of literature to explore and illuminate complex historical and cultural themes.

Day 2 in Belgrade: Shopping and Royal Families Residences Sightseeing

9:00 AM Start your day with a shopping tour at Terazije and Knez Mihailova. After having breakfast at your hotel, head to the Old Palace, which is now home to Belgrade's parliament. Located just around the corner from your hotel, you can stroll around Terazije, one of Belgrade's most famous squares. Be sure to drink water from the famous Terazije's fountain and soak in the spirit of old Belgrade, dating back to the 19th century.

Continue your tour to the Knez Mihajlova Boulevard, which stretches through Kalemegdan and is closed for transportation. If you're interested in art pieces, there are many galleries in Knez Mihailova that are free of charge to enter. You can also sit in one of the cafes and enjoy the atmosphere of the crowded boulevard. There are numerous shops where you can buy something for yourself or your loved ones.

12:00 PM Republic Square and National Museum: Head to Republic Square, where you will find the monument of Knez Mihailo. Visit the National Museum, which has great artworks by European and Serbian artists on display. For just 200RSD (less than 2 euros), you can see art works from ancient history up until the 20th century. The National Theatre is also located nearby.

3:00 PM Enjoy lunch at Dva Jelena Restaurant, which is located at Skadarska 32. The cost of a meal is less than 10 euros per person.

4:30 PM The Residence of Princess Ljubica: See this monument of culture, which is of exceptional importance as it is one of the most remarkable examples of preserved civil architecture from the first half of the 19th century in Belgrade.

6:30 PM Visit the White Palace (Beli Dvor) and King's Palace. Spread over 130 hectares, the White Palace, the King's Palace, and the surrounding park are worth spending your time and a bit of money on. The Serbian Royal family of Karadjordjevic resided here since 1936. There are also some great art pieces from Nicolas Pussen and other Serbian artists, such as Paja Jovanovic. The cost is 450RSD.

8:00 PM Have dinner at Kosmaj Restaurant, which is located at Cvijiceva 105. The cost of a meal is about 5-8 euros per person. Don't forget to try the cabbage rolls, which are called "sarma" in Serbian. It is the most loved meal in Serbia.

10:00 PM Return to your hotel and reflect on your experiences from the day.

Day 2 in Belgrade: Map

Below you can see the Map with the suggested activities for your second day in Belgrade. This map is accessible online in a Google Maps format, which will help you to navigate easily on foot, on bus, tram and car, when you are in the city.

You can get it at:
https://www.google.com/maps/d/edit?mid=zFotHPBWznGY.kKwV HvafVR_I&usp=sharing

[Click Here to Get This Map on Google Maps](#)

Do not miss the chance to try one of the Serbian specialties: **Karadjordje's steak**, made of rolled pork or beef meat and stuffed with *"kajmak"*-another Serbian specialty- which is cream made of milk, mostly similar to cheese.

One of the best places to try Karadjordje's steak is Dva Jelena (Two Deers)

Address: Skadarska 32| **Tel:** (+ 381 11) 7234 885

9:30 AM Start your day by visiting the famous Temple of Saint Sava. This impressive Orthodox church is one of the largest in the world and is located on the Vracar plateau, providing a great view of the city. Take some time to appreciate the stunning architecture and take panoramic photos of the city. The entrance is free of charge.

11:00 AM Head to Ada Ciganlija, a popular river island that is now a peninsula connected to the land by a bridge. You can take a swim if the weather is right or stroll along the promenade and relax in one of the cafes while enjoying the beautiful views.

2:00 PM Return to the hotel to freshen up and prepare for lunch.

2:30 PM For lunch, head to Zavicaj Restaurant and try the famous Serbian dish, kebabs (cevapi). The restaurant is located at Gavrila Principa 77 and offers a cozy and pleasant atmosphere. The cost for a meal is about 8 euros per person.

3:30 PM Visit the Nikola Tesla Museum, dedicated to the life and work of the famous Serbian inventor and electrical engineer. Nikola Tesla is considered one of the most important scientists of the 20th century, and the museum displays his inventions and contributions to science. The entrance fee is 500RSD.

5:00 PM Visit the Memorial Museum of Ivo Andric, the only Serbian Nobel laureate and renowned writer. The museum is located in his former apartment in Belgrade and displays artifacts and personal belongings of the writer. The entrance is free of charge.

6:00 PM Relax and enjoy nature in Pionirski Park, located just behind the Memorial Museum of Ivo Andric. Take a stroll and see the Watchtower of the Serbian High Command, which was transferred from Kajmakchalan to Pionirski Park.

7:00 PM Have dinner at Savamala, a famous restaurant located at Savski Trg 7. The menu includes traditional Serbian dishes such as cevapi, but also international cuisine. The cost is between 6-10 euros per person.

9:00 PM Experience the lively nightlife of Belgrade by heading to a traditional Serbian tavern such as Ispod Mosta. Try the famous sljivovica, a plum-flavored brandy, or other types of rakija with honey, apple quince, or apricot flavors. Afterward, continue the night out in one of the many clubs, raft discos, or taverns that Belgrade has to offer.

1:00 AM Return to your hotel and settle your impressions of the day before your next visit to the Serbian capital.

Day 3 in Belgrade: Map

Below you can see the Map with the suggested activities for your third day in Belgrade. This map is accessible online in a Google Maps format, which will help you to navigate easily on foot, on bus, tram and car, when you are in the city. You can get it at:

https://www.google.com/maps/d/edit?mid=zFotHPBWznGY.kcTp5t XHCIAI&usp=sharing

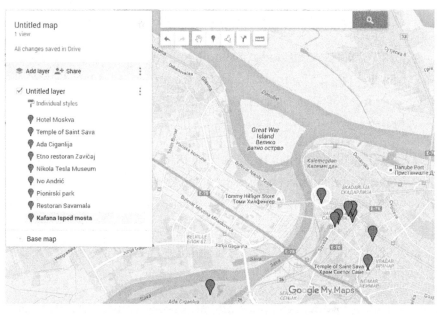

[Click Here to See this Map on Google Maps and Get the Directions](#)

ZoomTip 3.1 Taxi Fares in Belgrade

Belgrade has a well-organized public transportation system, but if you are in a hurry, taking a taxi is a good option. As mentioned, taxi rates in Belgrade are fixed, and there are many taxi associations to choose from. The starting tariff is 170RSD, and for every kilometer, there is an additional charge of 65RSD. If you are traveling on a Sunday or during the night, the charge per kilometer increases to 85RSD.

For example, if you need to travel from the airport to your hotel, the cost would be around 1400RSD, which is approximately 12 euros. While streetcars are a faster option for longer distances, taxis are recommended for urgent situations, as Belgrade's public transport can often experience heavy traffic.

It's important to note that while there are many reputable taxi companies in Belgrade, there are also some unlicensed drivers who may try to overcharge you. To avoid this, it's best to use licensed taxis or ride-sharing apps, such as CarGo or TaxiGo. These apps provide a fixed price for your ride and are generally reliable and safe.

Overall, taking a taxi in Belgrade is a convenient and safe option for getting around the city. With fixed rates and a variety of taxi associations to choose from, you can easily navigate the city without worrying about excessive charges.

See the list of Taxi Fares in Belgrade
See the list of Taxi Associations in Belgrade

General tips on Belgrade:

Here are some general tips for visiting Belgrade:

- If you're interested in historical and archaeological sites, consider visiting Vinca and Avala. Vinca is a significant archaeological discovery in Europe, while Avala offers a great panoramic view of Serbia from its TV tower. Visit the official website of the Belgrade Tourist Organization for more information on planning your trip (For planning your visit click here.)

- Belgrade is known for its vibrant nightlife, which includes a variety of options such as clubs, raft discos, and taverns. No matter what your taste is, there's something for everyone in Belgrade. Keep in mind that the party doesn't stop until the early morning hours!

- If you're traveling with kids, make sure to visit the Belgrade Zoo Park, located on Kalemegdan. It's a great place for families to spend an afternoon.

- Vegetarians may find it challenging to find options in Belgrade, as Serbian cuisine is heavily meat-based. However, some vegetable dishes like baked beans (prebranac) and cabbage (svadbarski kupus) can be found in traditional Serbian restaurants.

- Don't miss out on trying Serbian coffee, also known as Turkish or homemade coffee. You can find it in coffee shops and restaurants throughout the city.

- There are many other museums and monuments worth visiting in Belgrade, including the Museum of Contemporary Art (which has recently reopened), the Church of St. Mark, the Belgrade

Cathedral, and the Historical Museum of Serbia. These attractions have low-cost entry fees, making them an affordable way to explore the city's history and culture.

- For more information on planning your trip to Belgrade, visit the official website of the Belgrade Tourist Organization at http://www.tob.rs/en.

Thank you

We hope that this travel guide has helped you plan your visit to Belgrade, Serbia's vibrant capital city. Belgrade offers a unique blend of history, culture, food, and entertainment that is sure to leave a lasting impression on every traveler. From the city's impressive monuments and museums to its lively nightlife and delicious cuisine, there is something for everyone in Belgrade. So, pack your bags and get ready to discover the magic of this beautiful city. We wish you a pleasant journey and unforgettable memories!